INTRODUCTION AND SUMMARY

This report sets forth the results of a year-long investigation into the role of United States intelligence agencies with respect to alleged improprieties by the government, representatives and agents of South Korea in the United States.

The Committee's investigation was conducted as a case study of the activities of "friendly" intelligence services in the United States. The South Korean case was selected because it was the subject of considerable public attention and much information was already available. The Committee is equally concerned about similar allegations that have been made about the intelligence activities of some other friendly countries. The Committee will continue to seek to ascertain the extent of the intelligence activities of other governments with whom the United States has good relations as well as the U.S. Government's response to these activities.

The particular focus of the Committee, in examining the documentary record and interviewing key Executive Branch officials, has been on the extent to which the U.S. Government knew of the Korean government's activities, the decisions that were made, and the resulting actions which were or were not taken. The knowledge which the U.S. Government had, most of it based upon intelligence reporting, was extensive, detailed, and current.[1] That knowledge ranged from simple awareness as early as 1963 that the Korean intelligence service was monitoring the activities of Korean residents in the United States, to knowledge by 1971–73 that the Korean Government was attempting by unlawful means to influence and sometimes intimidate hundreds of Korean nationals who were living in this country. It included knowledge in 1971, not only of plans to improperly influence Members of the U.S. Congress, but also of unlawful payments that had actually been made that same year to members of the legislative branch to influence U.S. legislative action.

Most of this information was received by the United States intelligence agencies as a by-product of their routine foreign intelligence work. None of it was obtained as the result of specific levied requirements, and no intelligence agent was every directed specifically to focus on the subject in a comprehensive way. The U.S. Government never set as an intelligence collection priority the question of whether "friendly" foreign intelligence services were conducting activities directed at officials or other residents of the United States. Although much of the information received was disseminated to those components of the U.S. Government with law enforcement or foreign policy responsibilities, some pieces of relevant information were never passed on to anyone in a position to take action. The intelligence agencies' dissemination of the information was unfocused, haphazard, and without useful analysis.

---

[1] For purposes of this report, the Committee is assuming the reliability of the human sources whose information was being reported. A separate Committee study on the reliability of such information is now underway.

At no time before 1975 was a full and complete "package" ever presented to anyone within or outside the intelligence community reflecting the full scope, extent, and implications of Korean activity. Although over several years much of the information was disseminated on an *ad hoc* basis to various levels and components of the Government, it was not until 1975 that any senior accountable Federal official, though knowledgeable, addressed the problem in a comprehensive way.

The Committee believes that some of the information which was distributed was of sufficient significance to have merited earlier action. The Committee has examined the full record of the Executive Branch and has concluded that prior to 1975 no effective action was taken by anyone in authority to halt what was going on. Some concerned officials did bring the key issues to the attention of responsible Government authorities; however, those notifications were not acted upon in a manner commensurate with the magnitude of the activities involved.

The Committee has also investigated the question of whether there was an intentional "cover-up" by Executive Branch officials, and we have discovered no evidence to support such a conclusion. Viewed in the context of how the United States Government has generally handled relations with friendly foreign intelligence services in the past, the lack of effective and timely action is understandable, but we believe that new policies and new procedures must be devised to insure that this kind of problem does not recur.

This study did not address the question of the efficacy of U.S. counterintelligence efforts against hostile intelligence services in the United States. The recent indictment involving alleged Soviet intelligence activities in the New York City area dramatizes the continued gravity of that problem, and the Committee will specifically report on both the magnitude of the Soviet threat as well as the adequacy of the U.S. response in due course. It is beyond question that the activities of hostile intelligence services in the United States pose a more direct threat to the security of our nation and an even greater infringement on the liberties of our citizenry than do a few random, albeit intensive, operations by the intelligence services of our friends and allies. Indeed, it is the Committee's view that the amount of attention and resources required to be dedicated to the threat posed by hostile intelligence services could account for the lack of effective reaction in the Korea case.

In the past, our counterintelligence effort has focused upon the intelligence services of our adversaries, not our friends and allies. Perhaps, as one counterintelligence officer put it, "We have enough to do just trying to stay up with the KGB." Whatever the reason, it is clear that no means have yet been designed to prevent "friendly" foreign intelligence services from acting in ways that have and still could subvert our laws and subject our citizens to intimidation by foreign powers. Our intelligence agencies do not systematically ascertain the identities of and/or the assignments of agents or intelligence officers of "friendly" foreign governments who are in, or are coming to, the United States in "cover" capacities. Moreover, in cases where the United States Government becomes incidentally aware that such an officer is in the United States to fulfill an operational, as opposed to a liaison function, no steps are taken to determine the nature of that function unless there is some indication that he is violating United States law. The U.S. intelligence community does not command sufficient means, resources, or manpower to monitor the activities of "friendly" intelligence agencies' activities in the United States.

One of the key questions that must be answered is to what extent the United States Government should knowingly permit *any* foreign intelligence officers to conduct operations in the United States. The answer to this basic question is in part answered by our own need to conduct intelligence operations abroad. If the United States Government arrests or expels foreign intelligence officers or agents, then it risks foreign retaliation against U.S. intelligence operatives, innocent U.S. citizens, or the foreign policy interests of the United States. As the situation now stands, there are no formal rules, no written agreements, and no definitive limitations governing the conduct of intelligence services. Perhaps it cannot be otherwise. But, there must be a recognition that the issues and practices revealed by the Korean case have not been resolved, and unless they are, other cases of abuse will surely arise.

FINDINGS OF FACT

Within weeks after this investigation began, it became apparent that there were crucial issues to be dealt with which went beyond the question of when the U.S. intelligence community first became aware that agents of the South Korean intelligence service (KCIA) were engaged in efforts to improperly influence the U.S. Congress. A review of all available U.S. intelligence reports concerning the KCIA made clear that KCIA officials were "operational" in the United States as early as 1963, just two years after the KCIA was formed. At that time, the Department of State received a report from one of the intelligence agencies that KCIA officers had been directed to monitor the activities of Korean residents in Los Angeles and to solicit their support for the government of Pak Chung-hi. There is no evidence that any action was taken by any State Department official, nor was any concern expressed, at that time.

It is reasonable to assume that there would be public acceptance of the stationing of foreign intelligence officers in the United States for the purpose of liason with our own intelligence services to exchange information of mutual benefit. Accordingly, the 1963 intelligence reports raised for the Committee the immediate question of precisely what the practices are.

1. *The U.S. Government is not usually notified by most foreign governments when "friendly" foreign intelligence officers are assigned here.* Although our own intelligence agencies are aware of who their own liaison counterpart is, neither U.S. intelligence, nor any other part of the United States Government, ever receives routine notification of all "friendly" foreign intelligence officers who are assigned to embassies or missions in this country. Moreover, in those cases where our own intelligence liaison officers might incidentally become aware of the identities of "friendly" intelligence officers who are stationed in the United States, the U.S. Government is not usually informed, nor does the United States inquire, as to the nature of their duties and mission.

Routine accreditation forms are filled out by all foreign diplomats who are assigned here, but these forms contain no questions, nor any information, about whether intelligence functions are among their duties. Indeed, it appears that the policy question of whether such notification should be required has never been dispositively addressed by the Executive Branch.

2. *The question has not been formally addressed, whether foreign governments should be permitted to perform intelligence operations in the United States.* The Committee's study has revealed that the intelligence function is assumed. The issue of not permitting intelligence activities is not considered. In the words of one U.S. official responsible for accrediting foreign diplomats, "I am so conditioned to the pervasiveness of our own intelligence operations overseas, that I

(5)

would never presume to suggest that other countries shouldn't be able to perform a similar function in this country."

On at least two occasions, the Department of State has addressed the question of whether persons accredited as foreign diplomats should be permitted to engage in other nondiplomatic activities. For instance, several years ago, the Department was concerned about accredited embassy personnel devoting substantial portions of their time to nondiplomatic affairs such as attendance at American universities or participation in international organizations such as the International Monetary Fund. At that time, the Department of State circulated a "note" to all foreign missions which reminded foreign governments that one of the "criteria" for accreditation was a requirement that each diplomatic officer "devote his official activities fulltime to diplomatic duties." The "note" continued:

> * * * [T]he Department has learned of instances of persons who, although accredited as diplomatic officers, are principally, if not solely, performing duties under contract at or appointment with one of the international organizations with headquarters in Washington * * * [T]he Department of State views such arrangements as necessarily collateral and subordinate to the member's diplomatic duties. Therefore, should the Department learn in the future of further instances where an accredited diplomat is performing duties under a full-time contract or appointment with an international organization, or is about to be converted to such status, the mission will be expected to return all credentials of that diplomatic officer to the Department of State, and that officer's name will be deleted from the Diplomatic List.
>
> The Department wishes again to stress the importance placed on the performance of traditional and accepted diplomatic functions by a diplomatic officer while in the United States and to make clear that it will continue to be unable to consider for accreditation any person who is, or, during assignment in the United States, will be a student or trainee at or with any college, university, vocational school, military institution, or private or governmental foundation, or engaged in any other pursuit inconsistent with regular and accepted diplomatic functions. In the past some governments have selected officials for assignment to the United States who, following arrival and subsequent accreditation as diplomats by the Department of State, have entered upon an intergovernmental military training course or been assigned at a private research institution. This practice is unacceptable. Each mission should notify the Department whenever any of its officers terminates diplomatic duties to engage in academic pursuits and should at that time return appropriate credentials.

No note has ever been issued on the subject of whether accredited diplomats may be engaged in intelligence activities in this country.

3. *The permissible limits of lawful foreign diplomatic lobbying of Members of the Congress has never been set forth.* The following exchange between the Senate Foreign Relations Committee and the

Department of State occurred during hearings on ratification of the Vienna Convention on Diplomatic Relations in 1965:

> Question. *A diplomatic agent is to deal only with the foreign ministry or the head of state of the country of his mission. How strictly is this observed? To what extent do diplomatic agents try to influence the press, Members of Congress, and industrial leaders without going through the State Department?*
>
> Answer. It has long been established that as a general rule diplomatic officers should conduct all official business with or through the ministry of foreign affairs, exept as may have been otherwise agreed.
>
> Any case of flagrant breach of normal diplomatic practice by obviously improper contacts is dealt with by the Department by making the Department's disapproval known to the diplomatic mission concerned.
>
> Many diplomatic missions have press attachés and information officers whose principal duty is to deal with the news media. The Department considers that this is a proper diplomatic function, so long as the mission does not make statements or disseminate political propaganda which is objectionable to the United States.
>
> The Department is, of course, not fully informed of the nature and substance of all discussions concerning matters of policy which diplomatic officers have with Members of the Congress and with industrial leaders. Such direct contacts. as distinct from contacts by nondiplomatic representatives of foreign governments, have not occasioned any significant complaint.

A proposal was made by State Department officials to circularize a "diplomatic note" on the question in 1970, partially as the result of "improper" lobbying by South Korea. A draft "note", containing a warning that activities by foreign diplomats or consular officers intended to influence congressional deliberations on matters in which their government has a financial or other beneficial interest would be unacceptable to the United States was not approved by the State Department because of the "difficulty in arriving at an agreed text and the doubts of many desks on the wisdom of an indiscriminate approach to all embassies." Instead. it was concluded by State Department officials that questionable activities would continue to be dealt with on an individual basis. How those activities were defined or dealt with in the Korean case will be discussed in greater detail below.

4. *The absence of any precise delineation of what "friendly" foreign intelligence services may and may not do within the United States has resulted in a lack of clarity with respect to jurisdictional responsibilities of individual U.S. Government agencies. This in turn has resulted in ineffective coverage of "friendly" foreign intelligence service activities.*

Officials of the Department of State and U.S. intelligence agencies maintain that the Federal Bureau of Investigation has primary jurisdiction over the activities of foreign intelligence services within the United States. The FBI in turn has maintained that it is their basic policy "to conduct investigations only in instances where we receive allegations indicating an individual representing a foreign nation is engaging in activities in violation of our laws or otherwise constitutes a security menace." The State Department apparently presumed that the KCIA's activities in Los Angeles in 1963 would not have fallen into either category.

In 1954 the FBI did acknowledge that the presence of "friendly" foreign intelligence services in the United States posed potential problems; however, the concern which was expressed by the Bureau at that time focused primarily upon the potential threat to the U.S. security posed by possible hostile infiltration by a "friendly" intelligence service. Within the somewhat narrow context of that concern, the FBI in 1954 urged the Department of State and U.S. intelligence agencies to notify the Bureau "when information is received that an intelligence representative of a foreign government is coming to the United States." The Bureau's request went on to state:

> We would like to be advised in the event any agency sets up a liaison arrangement with such an intelligence representative and to be furnished with brief details of his approved activity. This information is needed in order to guide this Bureau in discharging its responsibilities and, at the same time, it will enable us to advise the appropriate agency in the event information is received that the intelligence representative is acting outside the scope of his approved activity. Similarly, any information concerning the activities of these intelligence representatives coming to the attention of any agency which would appear to be outside the scope of their prescribed activity should be brought to the attention of this Bureau. These data will assist us in eliminating unnecessary inquiries and in concentrating on those matters of this type which merit close attention.
>
> We would like to have this information with respect to intelligence representatives now in the United States and, on a continuing basis, with respect to future arrivals. Of course, we desire to continue to be furnished data concerning suspected intelligence representatives who arrive and with whom no working arrangement exists.

The Committee has examined the notifications which were received by the FBI with respect to South Korean intelligence officers. Most of those notifications related to Korean intelligence officials who were in the United States on official visits or as guests of the U.S. Government. In 1970 one of the U.S. intelligence agencies supplied the Bureau with a complete list of all South Korean intelligence officers who were then known to be in the United States, together with their "cover" designations. There is no indication that the Bureau ever took any action upon receipt of the list. We have found no evidence that any inquiry was undertaken to determine whether any of the intelligence officers on the list were acting "outside the scope of (their) approved activities." Most significantly, the Committee has found there is no written policy, guideline, rule or requirement available to the FBI or any other U.S. authority, which articulates what is and what is not considered to be "approved activity."

With respect to the question of whether the FBI should conduct an investigation to determine the activities of foreign intelligence officers stationed within the United States, Bureau officials have informed the Committee:

(a) Such an undertaking would be practically impossible because of the numbers involved. As one official observed, "We have enough to do just trying to stay up with the KGB."

(b) Such an undertaking would be an exercise in futility since no resultant action could or would be taken. According to the Bureau, for foreign policy reasons, it is difficult to limit visas even for known officers of the KGB.

Finally, although the Department of Justice administers a criminal statute requiring that a registration statement be filed by any person who "has received instruction or assignment in, the espionage, counterespionage, or sabotage service or tactics of a government of a foreign country", the Justice Department is not unusually notified (nor has it ever asked to be notified) about the presence of foreign intelligence officers in the United States.

5. *The Committee has also determined that intelligence requirements processes do not include directions to U.S. intelligence agencies to determine the identities and assignments of "friendly" foreign intelligence officers who are in or coming to the United States.* Accordingly, any information which becomes known to U.S. intelligence and thereafter to other agencies of the United States, is available only because it might be voluntarily supplied in addition to other U.S. foreign intelligence assignments. The Committee learned that in the South Korean case, even after specific information about KCIA illegal lobbying was received, no intelligence instructions were ever issued to develop additional intelligence on the same subject. In the words of one former overseas intelligence officer "my reports met with absolute silence."

6. *Extensive specific information about KCIA operations being directed against South Koreans living in the United States came to the attention of U.S. intelligence agencies between 1971 and 1973 and was reported by those agencies to the Department of State.* Although the information received in 1963 about KCIA monitoring activities in Los Angeles may have appeared to U.S. officials to have been rather benign, it was clear by 1971 that the KCIA had set out to effectively impede opposition to the Pak regime by South Koreans living in the United States. U.S. intelligence learned in early 1971 of KCIA plans to disrupt and destroy the National Association of Overseas Residents, an anti-Pak organization in the United States. When Kim Tae-Chung, the leading South Korean opposition candidate, was planning to visit the United States that year, U.S. intelligence learned of KCIA plans to investigate all his activities and to block his meetings with U.S. officials. All of this information was reported to the Department of State. Notwithstanding the KCIA's efforts, Kim was officially received by the Secretary of State "to demonstrate an evenhanded U.S. Government policy toward the Korean elections," but there is no evidence that any action was taken by the United States to bring the disruptive operations to a halt.

By mid-1973 U.S. intelligence was aware that the KCIA's operations in the United States had intensified to the point where the KCIA was trying to block anti-Pak demonstrations by all possible means. Korean associations were to be penetrated, manipulated and weakened by the KCIA, and demonstrators were to be intimidated. When Kim planned a return trip to the United States the KCIA even considered a plan to use criminals in the United States to kill him. This plan was reported by U.S. intelligence to the Department of State, which by then was receiving its own firsthand accounts of KCIA harrassment from Korean victims. News accounts of some of these incidents were appearing in the press, and finally, in mid-June of 1973, a high-ranking Korean Embassy official, Lee Jai-Hyon, resigned and sought U.S. permission to reside permanently in the United States. Lee's resignation received widespread publicity and he was quoted in the press as confirming that "KCIA operatives work out of the embassy and South Korean consulates across the United States and conduct illegal surveillance and intimidation operations against Korean residents here."

7. *The first significant action taken by the U.S. Government with respect to reports of KCIA harrassment occurred in August 1973.* Although complaints had been made earlier by the Director of Korean Affairs in the Department of State to the Korean Ambassador and the KCIA station chief in Washington, including an expression of concern for the safety of Kim Tae-Chung, the KCIA's operations continued unabated. Finally, in August, at the urging of the Department of State, an FBI investigation was begun, official protests about the size and activities of the KCIA mission in the United States were lodged with the South Korean government, and State Department officials persuaded the South Korean government to recall their KCIA station chief from Washington. The Korean Ambassador to the United States was told by the Under Secretary of State that the KCIA mission in this country "can have one and only one function, and that is liaison with our intelligence community."

The FBI's investigation did not result in prosecution, and it is unclear what the purpose of the investigation was intended to be. FBI files reflect that investigators were instructed "to determine if persons residing in the United States are carrying out activities on behalf of the South Korean government which would be in violation of the Foreign Agents Registration Act." State Department records indicate that the Department's officers were not necessarily seeking "the kind of evidence necessary for prosecution in court," but "enough information upon which we can draw a reasonable conclusion regarding ROK CIA activities in the United States." During consultations between representatives of the FBI and the Department of State, the Bureau had confirmed that it had had "strong reasons to conclude that the ROK CIA is indeed involved in efforts to intimidate and harrass Korean citizens in the United States, although evidence, as against allegations, is not easy to obtain." According to state Department memoranda of their consultations with the FBI, the Bureau was "sensitive to the fact that a foreign government is involved, and they are also concerned about questioning as to their justification for conducting such an investigation. As a result they have been proceeding rather cautiously and on a limited basis, utilizing as grounds for their investigation the Foreign Agent Registration Act, which restricts them to the nondiplomatic area."

8. *The FBI's investigation of KCIA harrassment was limited, did not include debriefing a key prospective witness, and was conducted without the benefit of all available intelligence information.*

The FBI's investigation, which did add some additional details of harrassment and disruption at particular demonstrations, as well as confirmation by FBI sources of KCIA involvement, was as limited and as cautious as the State Department understood it to be. When the investigation was begun, all FBI field offices were instructed to be guided by the principle that "[the] State Department has primary responsibility for policing the activities of South Korean diplomats in this instance and it is not desired that we undertake massive investigations of South Korean diplomats unless such appears absolutely necessary."

Not only did the FBI not "undertake massive investigations of South Korean diplomats," but the investigative record reflects that at no point did the FBI investigate *any* South Korean diplomat. FBI Headquarters also instructed its field offices that "In the event it becomes desirable that direct investigation of an individual diplomat be instituted, Bureau (Headquarters) should be expeditiously advised so that State Department clearance for such an investigation may be initiated." No such clearance was ever recommended or sought.

It is unclear to the Committee what kind of information might have persuaded the Bureau that such investigations were "absolutely necessary." It is not unreasonable to presume that the Bureau might have had such information in hand if they had questioned Lee Jai-Hyon, who said he had actually been present at meetings in the Korean Embassy when the disruption plans were being discussed by officers of the KCIA, and who could, therefore, have provided first-hand evidence of what he had learned. Yet, the investigative reports reveal that Lee, though available, was not interviewed. This investigative omission is of even greater significance in view of the fact that it later became clear that Lee said he had detailed firsthand knowledge about not only the KCIA's disruptive operations, but their lobbying activities as well. In fact, when Lee testified before the House Subcommittee on International Organizations in 1975, he provided what he said were details of a comprehensive nine-point KCIA program "to mute criticism of [President Pak's] totalitarianism and to buy supporters in the United States." He described the KCIA's plans:

> To seduce and, if possible, buy off American leaders—particular in Congress—who have had any kind of close personal contacts with Korea through the Korean war or business.

> *　　*　　*　　*　　*

> To regiment Korean communities in the United States by infiltrating with front men or undercover agents the established Korean residents' associations and by creating new ones where such associations have not yet been organized. The purpose was to control and manipulate the Korean communities through the planted officers of such organizations, to silence criticism of (President) Pak's repressive rule

by singling out and intimidating dissident members and to stage in the name of associations falsified campaigns of Korean residents' total support for (President) Pak before the eyes of the U.S. Government and people; * * *.

*   *   *   *   *

To intimidate "uncooperative" Korean residents in the United States through their families, relatives and close friends in Korea, to silence dissidents and to make silent ones more "cooperative."

All of this information would probably have been available to the FBI if they had questioned Lee in 1973. Yet, he was not interviewed during the FBI's investigation. FBI files contain no record which would account for this investigative omission, and the FBI agent who directed the investigation is dead.

It is also reasonable to assume that the Bureau would have determined that investigations of South Korean diplomats were necessary if it had had all the intelligence which had been provided by U.S. intelligence to the Department of State during 1971 and 1972. As noted above, that information made clear the KCIA's plans to intimidate South Koreans living in the United States, and additional intelligence on the same subject was sent to the Department of State the following year. Some of that new intelligence was not forwarded to the FBI either by the intelligence agencies or by the Department of State when it was first received. Nor was information pulled together and sent to the Bureau in 1973, when the KCIA investigation was begun. It is the Committee's view that the FBI was not supplied with substantial information which might have convinced the Bureau of the need for a more comprehensive investigation than was actually undertaken.

9. *Although the Department of State successfully persuaded the South Korean government to recall the KCIA chief from Washington in late 1973, the harrassment operations apparently continued.*

As noted above, State Department officers pushed for an investigation not necessarily for prosecutive evidence, but because they needed to have "enough information upon which we can draw a reasonable conclusion regarding ROK CIA activities in the United States." Protests to the Korean Embassy at the working level had proven unsuccessful, and it had become clear by mid-June 1973 that more forceful action was required. It is possible that the additional information produced by the FBI's investigation provided enough additional data to lead to the "reasonable conclusion" sought, so that senior State Department officials could be persuaded of the urgency of the situation. At any rate, formal action was taken at the end of August 1973 when the Under Secretary of State successfuly urged the Korean Ambassador to send home the KCIA station chief from Washington. It is unclear what the effect of this action was. Shortly thereafter, U.S. intelligence learned, and reported to the Department of State, that in the weeks and months following Lee Jai-Hyon's widely publicized resignation in June 1973, KCIA officers in Washington had been directed to (1) deny the allegations of KCIA harrassment, (2) carry on their activities more secretly so there would be no recurrence of a Lee Jai-Hyon affair, and (3) lower their profile by coopting other

Korean officials to do the necessary "contact work" with Korean nationals. At the bottom of one of these intelligence reports, a U.S. intelligence officer noted, "Apparently KCIA won't desist from operations among Korean nationals in the U.S. but is becoming more sophisticated." Indeed, two years later, U.S. intelligence was again reporting KCIA plans to monitor anti-Pak demonstrations in the United States, and to manipulate the political activities of Korean residents here.

10. *A three-month FBI investigation in 1971, which was prompted by reports of improper Korean lobbying, was limited in scope and was conducted without the benefit of all available intelligence information.*

In 1971, the Department of Justice directed the FBI to undertake an investigation to determine whether Tongsun Park and/or an organization called Radio Of Free Asia (ROFA) was acting in violation of the provisions of the Foreign Agents Registration Act. The investigation was initiated at the urging of the Department of State which forwarded information to support their "strong suspicions concerning certain of the key Koreans involved (in ROFA), the organization's link to the ROK CIA, and the possibility that it and its parent organization, the Korean Cultural and Freedom Foundation. are covers for ROK, lobbying efforts in the United States." The FBI's investigation, which consisted of a review of publicly available records and biographical data on a few of the principals, and an interview of the head of ROFA, was closed in less than three months for lack of evidence. The closing of the investigation was approved by Acting Attorney General Kleindienst in March 1972, based upon recommendations he received from the Justice Department's Internal Security Division. The "paper record" reflects that the closing was handled in routine bureaucratic fashion, and the Committee has discovered no evidence to the contrary.

Some of the information which had been forwarded to the Department of Justice by the Department of State never reached the FBI. Since much of the State Department's information was based upon intelligence reports, a decision was agreed upon whereby one of the intelligence agencies would prepare an intelligence summary and transmit their summary directly to the FBI. However, this procedure failed to take two important factors into account:

(a) The State Department had sent the Justice Department some of their own information which had not come from any of the intelligence agencies. That information was not included in the summary which one of the intelligence agencies agreed to prepare, and it never reached the FBI. Perhaps the most crucial State Department data which never reached the Bureau was the following information which was in the original State Department submission to the Department of Justice:

We know for a fact that Pak (Ton Sun) offered to contribute to the campaign funds of several Congressmen, (coincidentally just before the supplemental MAP appropriation was submitted to the Hill), and have suspicions that he has been involved in many other irregularities as a lobbyist.

(b) The State Department's submission had included information based on intelligence generated by an intelligence agency other than the one which was preparing the summary. The other intelligence agency's information was not included in the intelligence summary and did not reach the FBI. This information stated:

Pak Ton Sun, member of the Korean Cultural and Freedom Foundation, was believed to be a member of the ROK CIA which "has a club called the Georgetown Club in Washington, D.C." * * *. [T]he Club served as a "front" to channel campaign funds to Congressmen.

Although the intelligence summary which was forwarded by the intelligence agency to the FBI reported that the South Korean government had formulated, but had later "tabled" a plan which would have given Tongsun Park control over KCIA lobbying activities in the United State, it did not reveal that U.S. intelligence actually had precise knowledge of the plan itself, containing considerable detail regarding implementation, including the proposed creation of an ostensibly legitimate organization in the United States comprised of specifically identified Members of the House and Senate. Moreover, the summary did not contain known information about the relationship between Tongsun Park, the KCIA, and individual high-level officials of the South Korean government. The Department of State was not aware of the extent of detail which U.S. intelligence had with respect to the plan; and even though State had received some information about Park's KCIA and South Korean government relationships, the intelligence agency was not asked by State to include that information in the summary which was being prepared for the FBI. Nor was the information volunteered to the FBI by the intelligence agency preparing the summary. Indeed, officials of the agency who were preparing the summary were not told that the FBI investigation would include the activities of Tongsun Park and Korean lobbying in the United States.

Some officials of the intelligence agency which prepared the summary were receiving more specific information about improper lobbying by South Korea, the KCIA and Tongsun Park. These reports occurred after the original Park lobbying plan had supposedly been tabled. The more detailed information was forwarded by those officials to FBI Headquarters in three intelligence reports (separate from the summary) during the same period that the summary was being prepared; however, FBI Headquarters did not forward those reports to the Bureau investigators then conducting the inquiry. Those absent reports reflected that:

(a) Tongsun Park was definitely under the direction of the KCIA.

(b) A named Member of the House of Representatives had recommended to President Pak that congressional lobbying efforts in the United States should be handled by Tongsun Park.

(c) President Pak had agreed to have Tongsun Park act as intermediary "in the rice deal." Park's commission was expected to be about one million dollars, about half of which was to be used for Korean lobbying in the United States.

(d) Some of Tongsun Park's commission was paid by Park to a named Member of the House of Representatives.

(e) The same named Member of the House of Representatives had solicited campaign funds from President Pak.

(f) Two named staff employees of the House of Representatives were connected with the KCIA.

(g) Korean lobbying activities in the United States had included an alleged donation of several hundred thousand dollars to the Democratic Party in the 1968 election.[2]

The decision by FBI Headquarters not to use the above information in its investigation—indeed its decision not even to communicate it to its own investigators—was made, according to the FBI, at the urging of a subordinate officer at the intelligence agency which generated the information. Notations in FBI files reflect that that intelligence officer told his counterpart at the FBI that the information could be disseminated only to Attorney General John Mitchell and Special Assistant to the President for National Security Affairs, Henry Kissinger, and that "sensitive sources [are] such that no inquiries whatsoever may be made on the basis of information furnished."[3] The intelligence officer has confirmed that his superiors did place a limitation on distribution, but has said that neither he nor anyone else at his agency restricted investigative use. He maintained that such investigative restrictions are customarily handled, where necessary, by limitations specified in the body of the disseminated intelligence report as opposed to being handled informally on the telephone, as the Bureau files notations reflect was done in this case. Whether or not such a restriction was discussed, the reports themselves were distributed to both Attorney General Mitchell and Dr. Kissinger. The reports contained the FBI Director's statement that no investigation was being conducted because the originating intelligence agency "has advised that the source of its information is extremely sensitive and such as to preclude any investigation whatsoever." Dr. Kissinger told the Committee that he does not recall seeing any of the three reports which were sent to him. Mr. Mitchell recalls only the one report which was sent to him which mentioned congressional staff employees, and he recalls bringing that matter to the attention of the Speaker of the House. The Committee has been unable to identify anyone on the staffs of either Dr. Kissinger or Mr. Mitchell who might have seen the reports. The difficulty of determining who actually saw the reports is compounded by the fact that most of the distributed reports which were actually delivered to other agen-

---

[2] A few years later, U.S. intelligence also learned that the KCIA was investigating an "unconfirmed" report said to be circulating in Washington about an alleged substantial Korean contribution to the 1968 Democratic presidential campaign, and the possibility that persons in the Republican Party might use the information in retribution when the Watergate investigation was finished. Tongsun Park has testified that he contributed $5,000 or $10,000 to the late Senator Humphrey's presidential primary campaign in 1972, and $25,000 to the Nixon's presidential campaign the same year.

These alleged contributions are not within the jurisdiction of this Committee and have therefore not been investigated as a part of this study.

[3] The subject of how the need for secrecy sometimes operates as an impediment to effective law enforcement will be addressed in detail in a separate Committee report.

cies and officials, and which might contain notations indicating who might have read them, cannot now be located.[4]

Two other reports which were distributed containing equally significant information, which were based upon information received by FBI Headquarters from another intelligence agency, similarly cannot be located. Copies of those reports which were retained by the FBI contain information reported in 1971 that:

> 1. A named Member of the House of Representatives and a named member of his staff had been cooperating with the KCIA, and the Congressman had received "payoffs" for assisting the Korean government before a House committee.

> 2. A person whom the KCIA suspected was on President Nixon's campaign staff was involved in attempting to negotiate a secret foreign aid grant with the government of Korea which was to be handled outside ordinary congressional channels, and for which U.S. Government officials would receive "kickbacks".

Reports containing the information described in the first paragraph above were sent to Attorney General Mitchell and Dr. Kissinger. Reports concerning the alleged "kickback" negotiations were sent to Attorney General Mitchell and Assistant Attorney General Robert C. Mardian. Neither of the reports was investigated,[5] and none of the information was furnished to the FBI's investigators who were then conducting the inquiry which had been initiated by the Department of State. Each of the reports contained FBI Director Hoover's representation that the Bureau was "precluded from instituting investigation based solely on information received from such sensitive sources." No one reviewed that decision and, although Dr. Kissinger recalled that he received the report about the Congressman, he assumed that such a matter was the responsibility of the Attorney General, who, he was aware, had received a duplicate copy of the report. Mr. Mitchell does not recall seeing either of the reports. Both Attorney General Mitchell and Assistant Attorney General Mardian have denied that any of their decisions in the Korean case were prompted by a concern that an investigation of any Korean matter would necessarily also require an investigation of the alleged kickback negotiations involving a purported Nixon campaign aide.

11. *Substantial additional intelligence about improper Korean lobbying was reported in 1972. Much of this information was reported to the Department of State, but none of it was brought to the attention of the FBI.*

---

[4] Although the Committee has examined the originating agencies' copies of all reports which were disseminated, twenty-three of the actual documents which were distributed to U.S. policymakers about Korean activities are unaccounted for. The unexplained disappearance of these highly classified memoranda, letters and reports has been brought to the attention of the Attorney General and the Director of Central Intelligence by the Committee.

[5] Mardian told the Committee the report looked like a "pure con" job and "a hoax." A limited inquiry was undertaken by the FBI with respect to the alleged kickback only for the purpose of further identifying the individual described as being on the campaign staff. That inquiry, which consisted only of an FBI file search, did not produce any information indicating that the individual was connected with the campaign (and the Committee has no further information indicating that he was). The FBI's inquiry was requested by Assistant Attorney General Mardian following a telephone conversation he had with Attorney General Mitchell. According to FBI records, Mr. Mardian urged the Bureau to undertake the limited inquiry based on his oral request because protection of the source "must be afforded paramount consideration and he did not like the idea of paper containing material which might jeopardize the source floating around."

After the FBI's investigation was closed in early 1972, U.S. intelligence continued to report detailed information about what the Koreans were doing. That information was current and reflected a variety of plans, strategies, and activities designed to affect U.S. policy. For example, intelligence reporting in the spring of 1972 described Tongsun Park as President Pak's personal representative in arranging rice deals, identified the KCIA Director as personally handling the rice transactions, and confirmed earlier reports that the purpose of the arrangement was to raise funds for the KCIA. Moreover, intelligence reports at this time not only corroborated earlier reports that the Korean government had contributed heavily to the Democratic Party in 1968, but also reflected that the Korean government had now decided that they should be supporting the Republican Party.

By late 1972, U.S. intelligence became aware of the names of a number of Congressmen and Senators that the Korean government believed could be influenced. In addition, intelligence reports which were sent to Dr. Kissinger and to the Department of State discussed a major, new Korean lobbying effort which was to be financed by the KCIA for the purpose of influencing Congress, the State Department, the media, and Korean residents.[6] The reports also reflected that Tongsun Park has been directed by the KCIA to arrange for particular named congressmen to visit Seoul, where they would be interviewed and Korean newspapers would report their pro-Korean views. At about this time, U.S. intelligence also reported that the KCIA Director and other Korean officials were studying a proposal which a named Member of the House of Representatives had made to President Pak that a Korean-American civilian coordinating council be established and that it be managed by Tongsun Park.

None of the above information was brought to the attention of the FBI.

12. *Because there was no intelligence requirement levied for information about Korean lobbying, the reporting process was on occasion incomplete and often without focus.* Some intelligence reports were sent to the Department of State, some to the FBI, some to the National Security Council, and some to various combinations of these components. On one occasion, a decision was made that significant information should not be reported to U.S. officials who might have been able to take responsible action. In 1971, overseas intelligence officers informed their headquarters that the American Ambassador had been asking for specific information about South Korean lobbying activities. The officers had precisely that kind of information in their possession, namely President Pak's approval for a particular Congressman's proposal that Tongsun Park be permitted to handle Korean lobbying, anticipated use of Park's rice sale commission to finance the lobbying effort, and the Congressman's personal solicitation of campaign funds from President Pak. Accordingly, the officers sought headquarters' permission to brief the Ambassador and to assure him that all information which was forwarded to headquarters was being passed on to high-level officials at the Department of State. Head-

---

[6] Dr. Kissinger does not recall seeing this information and there is no State Department record concerning these reports. These reports are among the twenty-three missing distributed documents, see p. 15, fn. 3, *supra*, and the Committee has thus been unable to determine, from notations which might appear on these reports, who might have read them.

quarters replied that the information in question was not being passed on to State Department officials, and further, that the Ambassador should not be briefed.

Some of the available information was not reported to headquarters by intelligence officers and was not discovered until a search of overseas intelligence offices was conducted as the result of current investigations conducted by the Department of Justice and committees of the Congress. Other information, while forwarded to Washington, was not included in the intelligence reports which were prepared for dissemination. On one occasion, information which was handled in this manner and which identified Tongsun Park as being completely under the control of a particular KCIA officer was sent in by the field as "(a)n interesting sidelight not included in the intelligence report."

13. *Although, over a span of several years, much of the information about Korean activities was forwarded to the analytic component of the intelligence community, no analysis of the information was ever done and none was ever sought by U.S. policymakers.*

The absence of any thorough analysis or compilation of all available information may have been due to the fact that no requirement was ever issued for information about Korean lobbying. One overseas intelligence officer informed the Committee staff that he could recall no other case where the information he was reporting had met with such deafening silence at headquarters. Although on one occasion in 1971 the Director of Korean Affairs at the Department of State expressed his concern to intelligence officers about "the entire ROKG lobby efforts here via Tongsun Park, Radio Free Asia, the Cultural and Freedom Foundation" and expressed "a need to gather information on * * * the entire ROKG lobby here, through investigation," this expression was not considered to constitute a "requirement" because of the level at which it was communicated, and at any rate, was considered to be the responsibility of the FBI rather than a task for the foreign intelligence community.[7]

Moreover, as indicated earlier, even on the single occasion when a document which was called an intelligence summary was prepared—in 1971 when the State Department urged an FBI investigation of Tongsun Park and Radio of Free Asia—the only documents which were summarized were those which had been specifically identified by the Department of State. Intelligence material which had been supplied to the Department of State by other intelligence agencies, and even some of the State Department's own information was not included; no file search was conducted to pull together other relevant information; and current intelligence on the same subject was not included, but was forwarded to FBI Headquarters as separate independent items. Those separate items were never forwarded to the FBI's own investigators who were handling the case.

14. *Even though the Department of State was never provided with an analysis or summary of what the KCIA, Tongsun Park, and the Korean government were doing, officials of the State Department did receive individual intelligence reports about some of the lobbying*

---

[7] Precisely the opposite position was taken by the FBI when the Radio of Free Asia investigation was closed in early 1972. Bureau agents at the time recommended that "any logical investigation * * * should be initiated in Seoul in the form of monitoring ROFA broadcasts and determining activities and ROK government connections with KCFF and ROFA personnel there."

*plans during 1970–1972. Several complaints were made by officials
of the Department of State to the Korean government in late 1970
and early 1971 about Korean lobbying. Those protests did not address
the fact that the activities were being directed by South Korea's intelligence service, and there is no record that any definitive action was
taken to halt the intensified efforts which were reported in 1972.*

In October of 1970, the U.S. Ambassador to South Korea, William
Porter, discussed the subject of "Korean lobbying in Washington"
with the Korean Foreign Minister and with the Korean Prime Minister. He told the latter about the "circular note" which was then being
drafted by the Department of State on the subject which would urge
all foreign embassies in Washington to "stay within bounds," [8] Porter
also told the Prime Minister that "the best thing for the Koreans is to
ride along on the residual good will in Washington toward the ROKs
and stop sending amateurs to lobby on behalf of that organism here."
Porter specifically mentioned Tongsun Park as one of the people,
among others, he had in mind and added that "People involved in such
activity outside the Embassy in Washington are amateurs and harming
the ROK cause." The State Department's Director of Korean Affairs
also met several days later with the Political Counselor from the
Korean Embassy, expressed his concern about Korean lobbying in the
United States, also mentioned the proposed circular note and expressed
his particular concern about the activities of Radio of Free Asia.

In November of 1970, Ambassador Porter again raised the subject,
this time with President Pak, in an effort to "enlist [President Pak's]
support in restraining Korean lobbyists in Washington" which Porter
described as "creating irritation" and "counter-productive." A few
months later Porter also asked the KCIA Director to try to restrain
Tongsun Park, but reported that it had apparently "not had effect."

Unilateral action with respect to Tongsun Park was taken by Philip
Habib when the latter succeeded William Porter as Ambassador to
South Korea. Park's free-wheeling activities, including his arranging
for congressional visits to South Korea (meetings were often arranged
for the Congressmen with Korean officials without U.S. Embassy
involvement), had long been a source of irritation to several officials
of the Department of State. One such official once even urged arranging for Park's "recall to Korea", prophesying that Park's activities
"sooner or later are bound to get him and the ROKG into serious trou-
ble, and would jeopardize all we have been attempting to accomplish
with Congress." Ambassador Habib specifically instructed all members
of the U.S. Embassy staff to have absolutely no contact with Park.

*15. A full-scale investigation was finally undertaken in 1975 when
the President directed State Department officials to deliver a collection
of new information to the then Acting Attorney General,[9] and an
investigation was begun by the Department of Justice.* In February
1975, Assistant Secretary of State Habib brought to Dr. Kissinger's

---

[8] This is the note which is discussed at p. 7, *supra* which was proposed but never
sent.

[9] This submission too, was not complete in that it contained only information which had
been reported by one agency in the intelligence community. Not included was extensive and
more detailed information describing Korean "cover action" and "influence operations"
which had been reported by another agency on the same subject. It is the Committee's
understanding, however, that Federal investigators have since been given access to all
relevant information in the possession of all the agencies.

attention new information which had been received by U.S. intelligence reflecting "extra-legal" Korean efforts to influence Members of Congress.

Dr. Kissinger consulted with President Ford, and asked Habib for more complete information on the subject. In late October 1975, Mr. Habib received and provided Dr. Kissinger more precise information on the same subject. Dr. Kissinger again consulted with the President, who directed that the information be transmitted to the Acting Attorney General.[10] It was so transmitted in mid-November 1975.

16. *The Committee has discovered no evidence that Tongsun Park's relationship with U.S. intelligence officers or other Executive Branch officials affected the collection or reporting process or resulted in the U.S. Government's failure to halt the activities of Park or the KCIA.*

The Committee has examined the question of whether Tongsun Park ever had a relationship with any U.S. Government officials that might have affected their actions in this case. Park had met Dr. Kissinger, Attorney General Mitchell, Attorney General William Saxbe, CIA Director Richard Helms and Defense Secretary Melvin Laird on social occasions. One one occasion he had lunch with FBI Director J. Edgar Hoover in the office of Congressman John Rooney, and on at least one occasion he met Secretary Laird in the latter's office. However, there is no evidence that any of these contacts had any bearing upon any action taken or not taken by any of these officials with respect to Korean lobbying in the United States.

Mr. Park also knew former Attorney General Richard Kleindienst and met with him in Kleindienst's office on one or two occasions; however, their discussions occurred subsequent to the time when Mr. Kleindienst authorized the closing of the investigations of Park and Radio of Free Asia and there is no evidence those discussions involved U.S. Government action with respect to Park's activities on behalf of South Korea.[11]

The Committee has also examined whether Tongsun Park had a relationship with any of the U.S. intelligence agencies that would have influenced intelligence collection and reporting, or resultant government action. The Committee has determined that although Park did have some limited contact with U.S. intelligence personnel, he was never considered by U.S. intelligence agencies to have been an asset, and he never had any formal relationship with any of those agencies. There is no evidence indicating that Park's limited contacts with U.S. intelligence officers ever had an effect upon the performance of these officers or the agencies they represented.

Beginning in 1959 and for several years thereafter, U.S. intelligence officers met with Park on occasion to obtain information and/or to assess him as a prospective asset. In 1962, there was also intelligence interest in the possibility of Park's heading up a New York City place-

---

[10] In 1977 a newspaper column contained an allegation that in October 1975, when the House Intelligence Committee was openly considering contempt proceedings against Administration officials, "Congressmen were warned about Administration knowledge of illegal payments * * *" involving Members of Congress. The Committee has found no evidence to substantiate this allegation.

[11] After Mr. Kleindienst left the Department of Justice, he occupied space in Park's office building on a rent-free basis for two months. During that time Kleindienst served as Park's attorney for two months for a retainer of $4,000. There is no evidence that these relationships had been planned or discussed until after Mr. Kleindienst authorized the closing of the Park/ROFA investigation. Mr. Kleindienst has told the Committee that his relationship with Park in 1971 was not such as required him to disqualify himself from the case, and we have discovered no evidence to the contrary.

ment service for Korean students studying in the United States who desired employment in their homeland. Although this particular organization was never created, Park was involved in some of the negotiations which resulted in a $1,500 Asia Foundation grant to an organization in Korea which was also involved in student placement opportunities. Park has testified that he was unaware at the time that the Asian Foundation was in any way connected with the CIA,[12] and there is no evidence to refute his claim.

In 1967, Washington intelligence officials were told by their overseas officers that Park was thought to be "worthy of cultivation" and Park himself was apparently told that a Headquarters official would be calling on him and might want to see him occasionally. The suggestion was made that Park might be of interest because of his close relations with key Korean officials. There is no indication in intelligence files that this proposal was ever acted upon, although two years later an intelligence officer who had just retired did in fact contact Park and arranged a private dinner gathering which was attended by two other intelligence officials. It was Park's recollection that the dinner was arranged by an intelligence officer who had been asked "to look me up." There is conflicting evidence whether the dinner took place in Park's home or in a Washington restaurant. It was apparently followed by a "tour" of the George Town Club. The Committee has been unable to ascertain why the dinner was arranged, and there are no records on the subject in intelligence agency files. One of the officers who was at the dinner was en route to a new assignment in Saigon and asked Park to let him know if he learned of any Congressmen who might be coming to visit there. Intelligence files reflect Park's subsequent efforts to contact one of the officers concerned, but, according to the officer, "I never returned his calls."

Additional interest in Park was expressed by another intelligence agency which, in 1968, was apparently considering recruiting Park as a "spotter assessor" to be used to recruit and assess possible sources of foreign intelligence information, but there is no evidence that Park was actually used in that capacity.

During the period 1970–71, Park apparently had numerous contacts with the CIA station chief in Seoul, although their recollections differ as to the substance of their relationship. Park considered the station chief to have been a close personal friend and he claims that they exchanged considerable substantive information about Korean politics and political figures. The station chief recalls their meetings to have been of a purely social nature rather than substantive. There are no records in intelligence files reflecting what transpired between them. Park recalls receiving a case of liquor from the station chief on at least one occasion.

Park's activities in the United States first came to the attention of the intelligence community in 1962 when one of the domestic components reported that Park and his Georgetown roommate, Douglas Caddy, were forming "a new and hopefully potent international anticommunist youth organization," called the International Federation of Free Youth. The intelligence officer who reported this information noted that his source, a close associate of Park, had not asked for sup-

---

[12] The Asia Foundation was funded by the CIA from 1951 to 1967.

port or guidance, but had passed the information along because U.S. intelligence "should be informed of this type of activity from the beginning." Although the intelligence officer told his superiors he would "appreciate an expression of interest in pursuing the development," there is no indication in intelligence files that any further action was taken. Although U.S. intelligence funded various student organizations during the 1960s, there is no indication that this particular organization was ever utilized in any fashion by U.S. intelligence. Moreover, relevant intelligence components have informed the Committee that they have never had any relationship with Mr. Caddy.

The same intelligence source which provided information about the International Federation of Free Youth was questioned several years later about the George Town Club and Park's involvement in the Club. There is no indication of what generated this later intelligence interest in that subject, nor is there evidence of any response to the intelligence officer's request to be notified by his superiors if there were interest in access to Park through the source. Intelligence files do reflect that at about this time a proposal was made, but rejected, to utilize the George Town Club as an operational base.

The Committee has also ascertained that two former intelligence officers had business relationships with Park, one while he was still employed by U.S. intelligence and in fact in his "cover" capacity. Nevertheless there is no indication that Park was aware that the intelligence officers were or had been so employed, and no evidence that their relationships with Park had any effect upon the intelligance agencies' performance to Korea.

In his testimony before the Senate Ethics Committee, Park readily admitted to knowing several former intelligence officials, but the Committee has discovered no evidence that any of those relationships affected the handling of the Korea case.

Despite the contacts, both witting and unwitting, that Park had with intelligence agents from time to time, there is no evidence that he was ever asked (or that any intelligence officers who were in touch with him were ever asked to find out about) the nature and extent of his activities on behalf of the government of South Korea.

RECOMMENDATIONS AND CONCLUSIONS

(1) There should be a standing requirement for overseas national intelligence agencies of the United States to attempt to ascertain the extent and nature of all foreign intelligence service activities in this country.

(2) To the greatest extent possible, the FBI should be kept fully and currently informed about the identities and assignments of all foreign intelligence officers assigned to the United States.

(3) The Executive Branch should establish policy guidance which insures adequate coverage of "friendly" foreign intelligence officers stationed in the United States, consistent with FBI authority and with rights guaranteed by the Constitution and laws of the United States.

The Committee is aware from the Korea case that foreign governments might also seek to improperly influence U.S. Government officials through the utilization of "agents" who might not always be specifically or easily identifiable as intelligence officers. Investigations of such "agents" who might be citizens of the United States and whose activities do not violate United States law pose significant constitutional problems. The Committee is not recommending the investigative targeting of such individuals. Nevertheless, it is clear that considerably more attention must be given to this problem by both the Executive Branch and the Congress to devise a means to insure that the use of non-intelligence personnel by foreign governments is carefully controlled.

(4) The FBI should devote greater resources to their counterintelligence effort in order to be able to counter the threats posed by both hostile and "friendly" foreign intelligence services.

(5) The Director of Central Intelligence should insure that all intelligence information which is received concerning foreign intelligence activities in the United States is analyzed, assessed, and transmitted promptly to the FBI, the Secretary of State, and the Special Assistant to the President for National Security Affairs.

(6) The FBI and the Department of State should clarify their respective responsibilities concerning the activities of foreign intelligence services in the United States.

(7) The DCI and the Attorney General should continue the recently initiated practice of notifying the intelligence committees of Congress in the event Members of the House of Representatives or the Senate or their staffs have been targeted by a foreign intelligence service.

(8) United States intelligence relationships with the Republic of Korea are not based upon any agreements which would have permitted the objectionable activities which the KCIA conducted in the United States. Moreover, when the United States Government is able to learn of such activities, it has the option to thwart them, albeit at some risk to our own intelligence and foreign policy interests.

The Committee is concerned that U.S. Government officials should appreciate the full range of actions open to the United States Government to deal with the problems raised by activities of friendly foreign intelligence services in the United States.

The Committee is also concerned that whatever may have prompted Korean intelligence officers to believe that they could operate with impunity in the United States is probably no different from conceptions—or misconceptions—which serve as the basis for every nation's intelligence activities all over the world. We cannot address this kind of case merely from the perspective of whether foreign agents should be permitted to buy United States foreign policy. The issue is much more fundamental than that. It requires awareness that the KCIA was *operational* in this country as long ago as 1963 and consideration of whether *any* operations other than liaison should have been, or should be, acceptable. And the complexity of resolving that issue requires acknowledgement of our own intelligence activities on foreign, including South Korean, soil, intelligence activities which are of great benefit to the United States.

If we wish to prevent future cases of improper activities by friendly foreign intelligence services in the United States, but conclude that an outright ban would unduly restrict our own operations abroad, then we should try to fashion some method of governing these international practices. That effort has never before been made, and it would be naive to believe that the United States could unilaterally promulgate standards for the conduct of friendly foreign intelligence services. It is the Committee's judgment that the United States Government, in consultation with our friends and allies, might want to try to establish agreed, formal or informal limits on the types of activities conducted within each other's territory. Although international agreements could not reasonably be expected to prevent activities which, in their very essence, are intended to be secret and undetected, at least there is the possibility that the potential for possible abuse could be lowered. In addition, the United States Government should consider the selective use, in cases of clearly unacceptable activities, of unilateral actions which would make clear the limits on the types of activities by friendly foreign intelligence services in the United States which will be tolerated by this country.